Songs of Joy

THE WORLD PUBLISHING COMPANY

CLEVELAND AND NEW YORK

SONGS *of* JOY *from the Book of Psalms*

SELECTED, EDITED, AND WITH AN INTRODUCTION BY

LOUIS UNTERMEYER

Illustrated by Joan Berg Victor

Published by The World Publishing Company
2231 West 110th Street, Cleveland, Ohio 44102
Published simultaneously in Canada by
Nelson, Foster & Scott Ltd.
Library of Congress catalog card number: 67–13820
Special contents of this edition copyright © 1967 by Louis Untermeyer
Illustrations copyright © 1967 by Joan Berg Victor
Typography by Jack Jaget

In all cases, the language of the Psalms in this book is that of the traditional King James version. Not every verse of every Psalm has been included; following is a list of the verses as they appear in the Psalms selected for this collection:

Songs of Joy

AN INTRODUCTION

The Psalms are the oldest as well as the greatest anthology of hymns and sacred poems. Some of them are more than three thousand years old. No one knows who wrote all of them, but it is believed that many were composed by David, a shepherd-poet, the young giant-killer who lived a thousand years before the birth of Christ and became King of Israel.

The Book of Psalms has been called a collection of collections, for it consists of materials compiled during many different periods. It contains the expressions of many different minds—their deepest thoughts, their meditations, their impassioned hopes, their fervent prayers, their petitions for help in times of trouble. Some of the psalms were written for a people who were exiled from their native land. One of the most poignant and appealing is Psalm 137 with its unforgettable combination of sweetness and sadness:

> By the rivers of Babylon,
> There we sat down, yea, we wept,
> When we remembered Zion.
> We hanged our harps
> Upon the willows in the midst thereof.
> For there they that carried us away captive required
>   of us a song,
> And they that wasted us required of us mirth, saying,
> "Sing us one of the songs of Zion."

How shall we sing the Lord's song
In a strange land?
If I forget thee, O Jerusalem,
Let my right hand forget her cunning.
If I do not remember thee,
Let my tongue cleave to the roof of my mouth;
If I prefer not Jerusalem above my chief joy.

Most of the Psalms, however, are full of happiness. There is an elevating spirit even in the songs of lamentation. They rejoice in beauty, they celebrate the joy of living. The very word suggests this glorification, for in Hebrew the Psalms are called *tehillim*, which means "songs of praise."

The Psalms served many purposes. Before they were collected and became the heart of the Bible, they were used in the temples and sung as public worship. They also answered the needs of the individual and provided personal responses to situations in everyday life. They were a revelation of the feelings of a religious community as well as the favorite poetry of the people.

Parts of the Bible had been translated into English as early as the ninth century, but no portion of it was printed until 1525. It was then that the history of the English Bible began with the scholarly work of William Tyndale. It was followed by adaptations by various hands, but Tyndale's remained the favorite version and was the basis of the Authorized Version which lasted through the centuries and is the one we use today.

It was in the early part of the seventeenth century that the Authorized Version appeared. Called the King James Version of the English Bible, for it was published during the reign of King James I, it was the work not only of churchmen and scholars but of writers to whom the English language was rich and beautiful and, most of all, noble. There were fifty-four translators, and the list of learned men was headed by Lancelot Andrewes, dean of Westminster, of whom T. S. Eliot wrote, "Even the larger public which does not read him may do well to remember his greatness in history."

The King James Version appeared in 1611 when English poetry was in its glory. It was the age of Shakespeare and Jonson, a time of eloquence, and the translators gave the Psalms a splendor of speech which the English language has never surpassed. Of all the varied sections of the Bible, the Book of Psalms was not only the most poetically rendered but has remained the most beloved. In their blend of simplicity and nobility the Psalms spoke of, as well as to, every man and woman.

It is the essential poetry of the Psalms which gives them everlasting power. The ancient Hebrew poets did not use rhyme, but they gave their writings a decided rhythm. In the Psalms the rhythmical movement is particularly strong.

Many of them are a kind of free verse with three beats to the line. When they were sung, usually in chorus, they were accompanied by horns and string instruments, and the beat was emphasized by drums and cymbals. The choral singing is described in Ecclesiasticus, one of the added books of the Bible: "Then shouted the sons of Aaron, and then sounded the silver trumpets, making a joyous noise to be heard for a remembrance before the most High. . . . The singers also sang praises with their voices, and with a great variety of sounds there was made sweet melody. And the people besought the Lord, the most High, by prayer till the solemnity of the Lord was ended and they had finished the service."

The music of the Psalms was sounded not only by the combined voices and instruments but by the words themselves. Even when we read the words today, they retain their melodiousness, a music that is reinforced by the magic of the images. The images are unique, for they are both powerful and charming. We are stirred by the splendid whimsicality of:

> The mountains skipped like rams,
> And the little hills like young sheep.

We are enchanted with the vision of:

> If I take the wings of the morning
> And dwell in the uttermost parts of the sea,
> Even there shall thy hand lead me,
> And the right hand shall hold me.

We are roused by the magnificence of such a conception as:

> Let the sea roar, and the fulness thereof,
> The world, and they that dwell therein.
> Let the floods clap their hands;
> Let the hills be joyful together
> Before the Lord . . .

We are held by the thought of the universe speaking to us:

> Day unto day uttereth speech,
> And night unto night showeth knowledge.
> There is no speech or language
> Where their voice is not heard.
> Their line is gone throughout all the earth,
> And their words to the end of the world.
> In them hath he set a tabernacle for the sun,
> Which is as a bridegroom coming out of his chamber,
> And rejoiceth as a strong man to run a race.

We are startled by the majestic command:

> Lift up your hands, o ye gates;
> And be ye lift up, ye everlasting doors!

In the midst of confusion there is the quiet assurance that:

> We will not fear, though the earth be removed,
> Though the mountains be carried into the midst of
>   the sea,
> Though the waters thereof roar and be troubled,
> Though the mountains shake with the swelling thereof.
> There is a river, the streams whereof shall make glad
>   the city of God.

There is a dazzling glory in a concept of God:

> Who stretchest out the heavens like a curtain;
> Who layeth the beams of his chambers in the waters;
> Who maketh the clouds his chariot;
> Who walketh upon the wings of the wind;
> Who maketh his angels spirits,
> His ministers a flaming fire.

Rarely in all literature do we find so moving an utterance, so rich and resonant a language, such stupendous images. This is poetry at its peak.

The passages from the Psalms that follow have been chosen for this volume because they have a special affirming appeal. They vibrate with joy, a zest for all that is wonderful in the world. These songs of praise and thanksgiving are as inspiring today as when they sang themselves into the hearts of men and women thousands of years ago. They have never lost their power to gladden and gratify. They remain as beautiful and uplifting as they are timeless.

LOUIS UNTERMEYER

VIII

O Lord our Lord,
How excellent is thy name in all the earth!
Who hast set thy glory above the heavens. . . .
When I consider thy heavens, the work of thy fingers,
The moon and the stars, which thou hast ordained;
What is man, that thou art mindful of him?
And the son of man, that thou visitest him?
For thou hast made him
A little lower than the angels,
And hast crowned him with glory and honour.
Thou madest him to have dominion
Over the works of thy hands;
Thou hast put all things under his feet:
All sheep and oxen,
Yea, and the beasts of the field;
The fowl of the air, and the fish of the sea,
And whatsoever passeth through the paths of the seas.
O Lord our Lord,
How excellent is thy name in all the earth!

XIX

The heavens declare the glory of God;
And the firmament sheweth his handywork.
Day unto day uttereth speech,
And night unto night sheweth knowledge.
There is no speech nor language,
Where their voice is not heard.
Their line is gone out through all the earth,
And their words to the end of the world.
In them hath he set a tabernacle for the sun,
Which is as a bridegroom coming out of his chamber,
And rejoiceth as a strong man to run a race.
His going forth is from the end of the heaven,
And his circuit unto the ends of it:
And there is nothing hid from the heat thereof.
The law of the Lord is perfect, converting the soul:
The testimony of the Lord is sure,
Making wise the simple.
The statutes of the Lord are right, rejoicing the heart:
The commandment of the Lord is pure,
Enlightening the eyes.
The fear of the Lord is clean, enduring for ever:
The judgments of the Lord are true and righteous
    altogether.

VIII

O Lord our Lord,
How excellent is thy name in all the earth!
Who hast set thy glory above the heavens. . . .
When I consider thy heavens, the work of thy fingers,
The moon and the stars, which thou hast ordained;
What is man, that thou art mindful of him?
And the son of man, that thou visitest him?
For thou hast made him
A little lower than the angels,
And hast crowned him with glory and honour.
Thou madest him to have dominion
Over the works of thy hands;
Thou hast put all things under his feet:
All sheep and oxen,
Yea, and the beasts of the field;
The fowl of the air, and the fish of the sea,
And whatsoever passeth through the paths of the seas.
O Lord our Lord,
How excellent is thy name in all the earth!

IX

I will praise thee, O Lord, with my whole heart;
I will shew forth all thy marvellous works.
I will be glad and rejoice in thee:
I will sing praise to thy name, O thou most High. . . .
The Lord shall endure for ever:
He hath prepared his throne for judgment.
And he shall judge the world in righteousness,
He shall minister judgment to the people in
    uprightness.
The Lord also will be a refuge for the oppressed,
A refuge in times of trouble.
And they that know thy name
Will put their trust in thee:
For thou, Lord, hast not forsaken them that seek thee.
Sing praises to the Lord, which dwelleth in Zion:
Declare among the people his doings.

XV

Lord, who shall abide in thy tabernacle?
Who shall dwell in thy holy hill?
He that walketh uprightly, and worketh righteousness,
And speaketh the truth in his heart.
He that backbiteth not with his tongue,
Nor doeth evil to his neighbour,
Nor taketh up a reproach against his neighbour.
In whose eyes a vile person is contemned;
But he honoureth them that fear the Lord.
He that sweareth to his own hurt, and changeth
    not. . . .
Nor taketh reward against the innocent.
He that doeth these things shall never be moved.

XIX

The heavens declare the glory of God;
And the firmament sheweth his handywork.
Day unto day uttereth speech,
And night unto night sheweth knowledge.
There is no speech nor language,
Where their voice is not heard.
Their line is gone out through all the earth,
And their words to the end of the world.
In them hath he set a tabernacle for the sun,
Which is as a bridegroom coming out of his chamber,
And rejoiceth as a strong man to run a race.
His going forth is from the end of the heaven,
And his circuit unto the ends of it:
And there is nothing hid from the heat thereof.
The law of the Lord is perfect, converting the soul:
The testimony of the Lord is sure,
Making wise the simple.
The statutes of the Lord are right, rejoicing the heart:
The commandment of the Lord is pure,
Enlightening the eyes.
The fear of the Lord is clean, enduring for ever:
The judgments of the Lord are true and righteous
    altogether.

More to be desired are they than gold,
Yea, than much fine gold:
Sweeter also than honey and the honeycomb.
Moreover by them is thy servant warned:
And in keeping of them there is great reward.
Who can understand his errors?
Cleanse thou me from secret faults.
Keep back thy servant also from presumptuous sins;
Let them not have dominion over me:
Then shall I be upright,
And I shall be innocent from the great transgression.
Let the words of my mouth,
And the meditation of my heart, be acceptable in
    thy sight,
O Lord, my strength, and my redeemer.

XXIII

The Lord is my shepherd; I shall not want.
He maketh me to lie down in green pastures:
He leadeth me beside the still waters.
He restoreth my soul:
He leadeth me in the paths of righteousness
For his name's sake.
Yea, though I walk through
The valley of the shadow of death,
I will fear no evil: for thou art with me;
Thy rod and thy staff they comfort me.
Thou preparest a table before me
In the presence of mine enemies:
Thou anointest my head with oil;
My cup runneth over.
Surely goodness and mercy shall follow me
All the days of my life:
And I will dwell in the house of the Lord for ever.

XXIV

The earth is the Lord's, and the fulness thereof;
The world, and they that dwell therein.
For he hath founded it upon the seas,
And established it upon the floods.
Who shall ascend into the hill of the Lord?
Or who shall stand in his holy place?
He that hath clean hands, and a pure heart;
Who hath not lifted up his soul unto vanity,
Nor sworn deceitfully.
He shall receive the blessing from the Lord,
And righteousness from the God of his salvation.
This is the generation of them that seek him,
That seek thy face, O Jacob. Selah.
Lift up your heads, O ye gates;
And be ye lift up, ye everlasting doors;
And the King of glory shall come in.
Who is this King of glory?
The Lord strong and mighty,
The Lord mighty in battle.
Lift up your heads, O ye gates;
Even lift them up, ye everlasting doors;
And the King of glory shall come in.
Who is this King of glory?
The Lord of hosts,
He is the King of glory. Selah.

XXVII

The Lord is my light and my salvation;
Whom shall I fear?
The Lord is the strength of my life;
Of whom shall I be afraid? . . .
Though an host should encamp against me,
My heart shall not fear:
Though war should rise against me,
In this will I be confident.
One thing have I desired of the Lord,
That will I seek after;
That I may dwell in the house of the Lord
All the days of my life,
To behold the beauty of the Lord,
And to inquire in his temple.
For in the time of trouble
He shall hide me in his pavilion:
In the secret of his tabernacle shall he hide me;
He shall set me up upon a rock.

And now shall mine head be lifted up
Above mine enemies round about me:
Therefore will I offer in his tabernacle sacrifices of joy;
I will sing, yea, I will sing praises unto the Lord.
Hear, O Lord, when I cry with my voice:
Have mercy also upon me, and answer me.
When thou saidst, Seek ye my face;
My heart said unto thee,
Thy face, Lord, will I seek. . . .
I had fainted, unless I had believed to see
The goodness of the Lord
In the land of the living. Wait on the Lord:
Be of good courage, and he shall strengthen thine
    heart:
Wait, I say, on the Lord.

XXIX

Give unto the Lord, O ye mighty,
Give unto the Lord glory and strength.
Give unto the Lord the glory due unto his name;
Worship the Lord in the beauty of holiness.
The voice of the Lord is upon the waters:
The God of glory thundereth:
The Lord is upon many waters.
The voice of the Lord is powerful;
The voice of the Lord is full of majesty.
The voice of the Lord breaketh the cedars;
Yea, the Lord breaketh the cedars of Lebanon.
He maketh them also to skip like a calf;
Lebanon and Sirion like a young unicorn.
The voice of the Lord divideth the flames of fire.
The voice of the Lord shaketh the wilderness;
The Lord shaketh the wilderness of Kadesh.
The voice of the Lord maketh the hinds to calve,
And discovereth the forests:
And in his temple doth every one speak of his glory.
The Lord sitteth upon the flood;
Yea, the Lord sitteth King for ever.
The Lord will give strength unto his people;
The Lord will bless his people with peace.

XXXIII

Rejoice in the Lord, O ye righteous:
For praise is comely for the upright.
Praise the Lord with harp:
Sing unto him with the psaltery
And an instrument of ten strings.
Sing unto him a new song;
Play skilfully with a loud noise.
For the word of the Lord is right;
And all his works are done in truth.
He loveth righteousness and judgment:
The earth is full of the goodness of the Lord.
By the word of the Lord were the heavens made;
And all the host of them by the breath of his mouth.
He gathereth the waters of the sea
Together as an heap:
He layeth up the depth in storehouses.
Let all the earth fear the Lord:
Let all the inhabitants of the world
Stand in awe of him.
For he spake, and it was done;
He commanded, and it stood fast.
The Lord bringeth the counsel of the heathen to
nought:
He maketh the devices of the people of none effect.

The counsel of the Lord standeth for ever,
The thoughts of his heart to all generations.
Blessed is the nation whose God is the Lord;
And the people whom he hath chosen
For his own inheritance.
The Lord looketh from heaven;
He beholdeth all the sons of men.
From the place of his habitation
He looketh upon all the inhabitants of the earth.
He fashioneth their hearts alike;
He considereth all their works.
There is no king saved by the multitude of an host:
A mighty man is not delivered by much strength.
An horse is a vain thing for safety:
Neither shall he deliver any by his great strength.
Behold, the eye of the Lord
Is upon them that fear him,
Upon them that hope in his mercy;
To deliver their soul from death,
And to keep them alive in famine.
Our soul waiteth for the Lord:
He is our help and our shield.
For our heart shall rejoice in him,
Because we have trusted in his holy name.
Let thy mercy, O Lord, be upon us,
According as we hope in thee.

XXXVI

Thy mercy, O Lord, is in the heavens;
And thy faithfulness reacheth unto the clouds.
Thy righteousness is like the great mountains;
Thy judgments are a great deep:
O Lord, thou preservest man and beast.
How excellent is thy lovingkindness, O God!
Therefore the children of men put their trust
Under the shadow of thy wings.

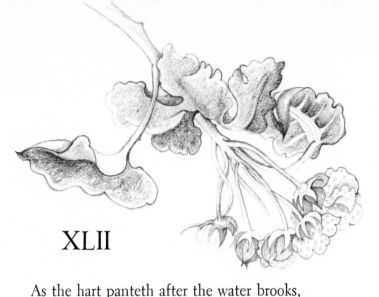

XLII

As the hart panteth after the water brooks,
So panteth my soul after thee, O God.
My soul thirsteth for God, for the living God:
When shall I come and appear before God?
My tears have been my meat day and night,
While they continually say unto me, Where is thy
    God?
When I remember these things, I pour out my soul
    in me . . .
Deep calleth unto deep at the noise of thy water-
    spouts:
All thy waves and thy billows are gone over me.
Yet the Lord will command
His lovingkindness in the daytime,
And in the night his song shall be with me,
And my prayer unto the God of my life.

XLVI

God is our refuge and strength,
A very present help in trouble.
Therefore will not we fear, though the earth be
    removed,
And though the mountains be carried into the midst
    of the sea;
Though the waters thereof roar and be troubled,
Though the mountains shake with the swelling
    thereof. Selah.
There is a river, the streams whereof
Shall make glad the city of God,
The holy place of the tabernacles of the most High.
God is in the midst of her; she shall not be moved:
God shall help her, and that right early . . .
What desolations he hath made in the earth.
He maketh wars to cease unto the end of the earth;
He breaketh the bow, and cutteth the spear in sunder;
He burneth the chariot in the fire.
Be still, and know that I am God:
I will be exalted among the heathen,
I will be exalted in the earth.
The Lord of hosts is with us;
The God of Jacob is our refuge. Selah.

XLVII

O clap your hands, all ye people;
Shout unto God with the voice of triumph. . . .
God is gone up with a shout,
The Lord with the sound of a trumpet.
Sing praises to God, sing praises:
Sing praises unto our King, sing praises.
For God is the King of all the earth:
Sing ye praises with understanding.

LXXIV

For God is my King of old,
Working salvation in the midst of the earth.
Thou didst divide the sea by thy strength:
Thou brakest the heads of the dragons in the waters.
Thou brakest the heads of leviathan in pieces,
And gavest him to be meat
To the people inhabiting the wilderness.
Thou didst cleave the fountain and the flood:
Thou driedst up mighty rivers.
The day is thine,
The night also is thine:
Thou hast prepared the light and the sun.
Thou hast set all the borders of the earth:
Thou hast made summer and winter.

XLVII

O clap your hands, all ye people;
Shout unto God with the voice of triumph. . . .
God is gone up with a shout,
The Lord with the sound of a trumpet.
Sing praises to God, sing praises:
Sing praises unto our King, sing praises.
For God is the King of all the earth:
Sing ye praises with understanding.

LXV

Praise waiteth for thee, O God, in Sion:
And unto thee shall the vow be performed.
O thou that hearest prayer,
Unto thee shall all flesh come.
Iniquities prevail against me:
As for our transgressions, thou shalt purge them away.
Blessed is the man whom thou choosest,
And causest to approach unto thee,
That he may dwell in thy courts:
We shall be satisfied with the goodness of thy house,
Even of thy holy temple.
By terrible things in righteousness wilt thou answer us,
O God of our salvation;
Who art the confidence of all the ends of the earth,
And of them that are afar off upon the sea:
Which by his strength setteth fast the mountains;
Being girded with power:
Which stilleth the noise of the seas,
The noise of their waves,
And the tumult of the people.

They also that dwell in the uttermost parts
Are afraid at thy tokens:
Thou makest the outgoings
Of the morning and evening to rejoice.
Thou visitest the earth, and waterest it:
Thou greatly enrichest it
With the river of God, which is full of water:
Thou preparest them corn, when thou hast so
　　provided for it.
Thou waterest the ridges thereof abundantly:
Thou settlest the furrows thereof:
Thou makest it soft with showers:
Thou blessest the springing thereof.
Thou crownest the year with thy goodness;
And thy paths drop fatness.
They drop upon the pastures of the wilderness:
And the little hills rejoice on every side.
The pastures are clothed with flocks;
The valleys also are covered over with corn;
They shout for joy, they also sing.

LXXIV

For God is my King of old,
Working salvation in the midst of the earth.
Thou didst divide the sea by thy strength:
Thou brakest the heads of the dragons in the waters.
Thou brakest the heads of leviathan in pieces,
And gavest him to be meat
To the people inhabiting the wilderness.
Thou didst cleave the fountain and the flood:
Thou driedst up mighty rivers.
The day is thine,
The night also is thine:
Thou hast prepared the light and the sun.
Thou hast set all the borders of the earth:
Thou hast made summer and winter.

LXXXI

Sing aloud unto God our strength:
Make a joyful noise unto the God of Jacob.
Take a psalm, and bring hither the timbrel,
The pleasant harp with the psaltery.
Blow up the trumpet in the new moon,
In the time appointed, on our solemn feast day.
For this was a statute for Israel,
And a law of the God of Jacob. . . .
Hear, O my people, and I will testify unto thee:
O Israel, if thou wilt hearken unto me;
There shall no strange god be in thee;
Neither shalt thou worship any strange god.
I am the Lord thy God,
Which brought thee out of the land of Egypt:
Open thy mouth wide,
And I will fill it.

LXXXIV

How amiable are thy tabernacles,
O Lord of hosts!
My soul longeth, yea, even fainteth
For the courts of the Lord:
My heart and my flesh crieth out for the living God.

Yea, the sparrow hath found an house,
And the swallow a nest for herself,
Where she may lay her young.
Even thine altars, O Lord of hosts,
My King, and my God.
Blessed are they that dwell in thy house:
They will still be praising thee. Selah.
Blessed is the man whose strength is in thee;
In whose heart are the ways of them.
Who passing through the valley of Baca make it a
    well;
The rain also filleth the pools.
They go from strength to strength,
Every one of them in Zion appeareth before God.
O Lord God of hosts, hear my prayer:
Give ear, O God of Jacob. Selah.
Behold, O God our shield,
And look upon the face of thine anointed.
For a day in thy courts is better than a thousand.
I had rather be a doorkeeper in the house of my God,
Than to dwell in the tents of wickedness.
For the Lord God is a sun and shield:
The Lord will give grace and glory:
No good thing will he withhold from them that walk
    uprightly.
O Lord of hosts,
Blessed is the man that trusteth in thee.

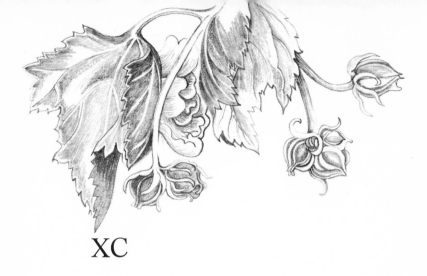

XC

Lord, thou hast been our dwelling place
In all generations.
Before the mountains were brought forth,
Or ever thou hadst formed the earth and the world,
Even from everlasting to everlasting, thou art God.
Thou turnest man to destruction;
And sayest, Return ye children of men.
For a thousand years in thy sight
Are but as yesterday when it is past,
And as a watch in the night.
Thou carriest them away as with a flood;
They are as a sleep:
In the morning they are like grass which groweth up.
In the morning it flourisheth, and groweth up;
In the evening it is cut down, and withereth. . . .
We spend our years as a tale that is told.
The days of our years are threescore years and ten;

And if by reason of strength they be fourscore years,
Yet is their strength labour and sorrow;
For it is soon cut off, and we fly away.
Who knoweth the power of thine anger?
Even according to thy fear, so is thy wrath.
So teach us to number our days,
That we may apply our hearts unto wisdom.
Return, O Lord, how long?
And let it repent thee concerning thy servants.
O satisfy us early with thy mercy;
That we may rejoice and be glad all our days.
Make us glad according to the days
Wherein thou hast afflicted us,
And the years wherein we have seen evil.
Let thy work appear unto thy servants,
And thy glory unto their children.
And let the beauty of the Lord our God be upon us:
And establish thou the work of our hands upon us;
Yea, the work of our hands establish thou it.

XCI

He that dwelleth in the secret place of the most High
Shall abide under the shadow of the Almighty.
I will say of the Lord, He is my refuge and my
    fortress:
My God; in him will I trust.
Surely he shall deliver thee from the snare of the
    fowler,
And from the noisome pestilence.
He shall cover thee with his feathers,
And under his wings shalt thou trust:
His truth shall be thy shield and buckler.
Thou shalt not be afraid for the terror by night;
Nor for the arrow that flieth by day;
Nor for the pestilence that walketh in darkness;
Nor for the destruction that wasteth at noonday.
A thousand shall fall at thy side,
And ten thousand at thy right hand;
But it shall not come nigh thee.
Only with thine eyes shalt thou behold
And see the reward of the wicked.
Because thou hast made the Lord, which is my refuge,
Even the most High, thy habitation;
There shall no evil befall thee,
Neither shall any plague come nigh thy dwelling.
For he shall give his angels charge over thee,

To keep thee in all thy ways.
They shall bear thee up in their hands,
Lest thou dash thy foot against a stone.
Thou shalt tread upon the lion and adder:
The young lion and the dragon shalt thou trample
    under feet.
Because he hath set his love upon me,
Therefore will I deliver him:
I will set him on high, because he hath known my
    name.
He shall call upon me, and I will answer him:
I will be with him in trouble;
I will deliver him, and honour him.
With long life will I satisfy him,
And shew him my salvation.

XCII

It is a good thing to give thanks unto the Lord,
And to sing praises unto thy name, O most High:
To shew forth thy lovingkindness in the morning,
And thy faithfulness every night,
Upon an instrument of ten strings,
And upon the psaltery;
Upon the harp with a solemn sound.
For thou, Lord, hast made me glad through thy work:
I will triumph in the works of thy hands.
O Lord, how great are thy works!
And thy thoughts are very deep. . . .
The righteous shall flourish like the palm tree:
He shall grow like a cedar in Lebanon.
Those that be planted in the house of the Lord
Shall flourish in the courts of our God.
They shall bring forth fruits in old age;
They shall be fat and flourishing;
To shew that the Lord is upright:
He is my rock, and there is no unrighteousness in him.

XCV

O come, let us sing unto the Lord:
Let us make a joyful noise to the rock of our salvation.
Let us come before his presence with thanksgiving,
And make a joyful noise unto him with psalms.
For the Lord is a great God,
And a great King above all gods.
In his hand are the deep places of the earth:
The strength of the hills is his also.
The sea is his, and he made it:
And his hands formed the dry land.
O come, let us worship and bow down:
Let us kneel before the Lord our maker.
For he is our God;
And we are the people of his pasture,
And the sheep of his hand. . . .

XCVI

O sing unto the Lord a new song:
Sing unto the Lord, all the earth.
Sing unto the Lord, bless his name;
Shew forth his salvation from day to day.
Declare his glory among the heathen,
His wonders among all people.
For the Lord is great, and greatly to be praised:
He is to be feared above all gods.
For all the gods of the nations are idols:
But the Lord made the heavens.
Honour and majesty are before him:
Strength and beauty are in his sanctuary.
Give unto the Lord, O ye kindreds of the people,
Give unto the Lord glory and strength.
Give unto the Lord the glory due unto his name:
Bring an offering, and come into his courts.
O worship the Lord in the beauty of holiness:
Fear before him, all the earth.
Say among the heathen that the Lord reigneth:
The world also shall be established that it shall not be
    moved:
He shall judge the people righteously.
Let the heavens rejoice, and let the earth be glad;
Let the sea roar, and the fulness thereof.
Let the field be joyful, and all that is therein:

Then shall all the trees of the wood rejoice before the
   Lord:
For he cometh, for he cometh to judge the earth:
He shall judge the world with righteousness,
And the people with his truth.

XCVIII

O sing unto the Lord a new song;
For he hath done marvellous things:
His right hand, and his holy arm,
Hath gotten him the victory.
The Lord hath made known his salvation:
His righteousness hath he openly shewed
In the sight of the heathen.
He hath remembered his mercy and his truth
Toward the house of Israel:
All the ends of the earth have seen
The salvation of our God.
Make a joyful noise unto the Lord, all the earth:
Make a loud noise, and rejoice, and sing praise.
Sing unto the Lord with the harp,
With the harp, and the voice of a psalm.
With trumpets and sound of cornet
Make a joyful noise before the Lord, the King.
Let the sea roar, and the fulness thereof;
The world, and they that dwell therein.
Let the floods clap their hands:
Let the hills be joyful together
Before the Lord; for he cometh to judge the earth:
With righteousness shall he judge the world,
And the people with equity.

CII

Hear my prayer, O Lord,
And let my cry come unto thee.
Hide not thy face from me
In the day when I am in trouble;
Incline thine ear unto me:
In the day when I call answer me speedily.
For my days are consumed like smoke,
And my bones are burned as an hearth.
My heart is smitten, and withered like grass;
So that I forget to eat my bread.
By reason of the voice of my groaning
My bones cleave to my skin.
I am like a pelican of the wilderness:
I am like an owl of the desert.
I watch, and am as a sparrow
Alone upon the house top.
Mine enemies reproach me all the day;
And they that are mad against me are sworn against
    me.
For I have eaten ashes like bread,
And mingled my drink with weeping,
Because of thine indignation and thy wrath:
For thou hast lifted me up, and cast me down.
My days are like a shadow that declineth;
And I am withered like grass.

But thou, O Lord, shalt endure for ever;
And thy remembrance unto all generations.
Thou shalt arise, and have mercy upon Zion:
For the time to favour her, yea, the set time, is come.
For thy servants take pleasure in her stones,
And favour the dust thereof.
So the heathen shall fear the name of the Lord,
And all the kings of the earth thy glory.
When the Lord shall build up Zion,
He shall appear in his glory.
He will regard the prayer of the destitute,
And not despise their prayer.
This shall be written for the generation to come:
And the people which shall be created
Shall praise the Lord.

CIII

Like as a father pitieth his children,
So the Lord pitieth them that fear him.
For he knoweth our frame;
He remembereth that we are dust.
As for man, his days are as grass:
As a flower of the field, so he flourisheth.
For the wind passeth over it, and it is gone;
And the place thereof shall know it no more.
But the mercy of the Lord is from everlasting to ever-
  lasting
Upon them that fear him,
And his righteousness unto children's children;
To such as keep his covenant . . .

CIV

Bless the Lord, O my soul.
O Lord my God, thou art very great;
Thou art clothed with honour and majesty.
Who coverest thyself with light as with a garment:
Who stretchest out the heavens like a curtain:
Who layeth the beams of his chambers in the waters:
Who maketh the clouds his chariot:
Who walketh upon the wings of the wind:
Who maketh his angels spirits;
His ministers a flaming fire:
Who laid the foundations of the earth,
That it should not be removed for ever.
Thou coveredst it with the deep as with a garment:
The waters stood above the mountains.
At thy rebuke they fled;
At the voice of thy thunder they hasted away.
They go up by the mountains; they go down by the
    valleys
Unto the place which thou hast founded for them.
Thou hast set a bound that they may not pass over;
That they turn not again to cover the earth.
He sendeth the springs into the valleys,
Which run among the hills.
They give drink to every beast of the field:
The wild asses quench their thirst.

By them shall the fowls of the heaven
Have their habitation,
Which sing among the branches.
He watereth the hills from his chambers:
The earth is satisfied with the fruit of thy works.
He causeth the grass to grow for the cattle,
And herb for the service of man:
That he may bring forth food out of the earth . . .
The glory of the Lord shall endure for ever:
The Lord shall rejoice in his works.
He looketh on the earth, and it trembleth:
He toucheth the hills, and they smoke.
I will sing unto the Lord as long as I live:
I will sing praise to my God while I have my being.
My meditation of him shall be sweet:
I will be glad in the Lord.
Let the sinners be consumed out of the earth,
And let the wicked be no more.
Bless thou the Lord, O my soul.
Praise ye the Lord.

CXVII

O praise the Lord, all ye nations:
Praise him, all ye people.
For his merciful kindness is great toward us:
And the truth of the Lord endureth for ever.
Praise ye the Lord.

CXXI

I will lift up mine eyes unto the hills,
From whence cometh my help.
My help cometh from the Lord,
Which made heaven and earth.
He will not suffer thy foot to be moved:
He that keepeth thee will not slumber.
Behold, he that keepeth Israel
Shall neither slumber nor sleep.
The Lord is thy keeper:
The Lord is thy shade upon thy right hand.
The sun shall not smite thee by day,
Nor the moon by night.
The Lord shall preserve thee from all evil:
He shall preserve thy soul.
The Lord shall preserve thy going out and thy com-
    ing in
From this time forth, and even for evermore.

CXXXIX

O Lord, thou hast searched me, and known me.
Thou knowest my downsitting and mine uprising,
Thou understandest my thought afar off.
Thou compassest my path and my lying down,
And art acquainted with all my ways. . . .
If I ascend up into heaven, thou art there:
If I make my bed in hell, behold, thou art there.
If I take the wings of the morning
And dwell in the uttermost parts of the sea;
Even there shall thy hand lead me,
And thy right hand shall hold me.

CXLIV

Lord, what is man, that thou takest knowledge of him!
Or the son of man, that thou makest account of him!
Man is like to vanity:
His days are as a shadow that passeth away.
Bow thy heavens, O Lord, and come down:
Touch the mountains, and they shall smoke.
Cast forth lightning, and scatter them:
Shoot out thine arrows, and destroy them.

CXLVII

Praise ye the Lord:
For it is good to sing praises unto our God;
For it is pleasant; and praise is comely.
The Lord doth build up Jerusalem:
He gathereth together the outcasts of Israel.
He healeth the broken in heart,
And bindeth up their wounds.
He telleth the number of the stars;
He calleth them all by their names.
Great is our Lord, and of great power:
His understanding is infinite.
The Lord lifteth up the meek:
He casteth the wicked down to the ground.
Sing unto the Lord with thanksgiving;
Sing praise upon the harp unto our God:
Who covereth the heaven with clouds,
Who prepareth rain for the earth,
Who maketh grass to grow upon the mountains.
He giveth to the beast his food,
And to the young ravens which cry.
He delighteth not in the strength of the horse:
He taketh not pleasure in the legs of a man.
The Lord taketh pleasure in them that fear him,
In those that hope in his mercy.

Praise the Lord, O Jerusalem;
Praise thy God, O Zion.
For he hath strengthened the bars of thy gates;
He hath blessed thy children within thee.
He maketh peace in thy borders,
And filleth thee with the finest of the wheat.
He sendeth forth his commandment upon earth:
His word runneth very swiftly.
He giveth snow like wool:
He scattereth the hoarfrost like ashes.
He casteth forth his ice like morsels:
Who can stand before his cold?
He sendeth out his word, and melteth them:
He causeth his wind to blow, and the waters to flow.
He sheweth his word unto Jacob,
His statutes and his judgments unto Israel.
He hath not dealt so with any nation:
And as for his judgments, they have not known them.
Praise ye the Lord.

CXLVIII

Praise ye the Lord.
Praise ye the Lord from the heavens:
Praise him in the heights.
Praise ye him, all his angels:
Praise ye him, all his hosts.
Praise ye him, sun and moon:
Praise him, all ye stars of light.

Praise him, ye heavens of heavens,
And ye waters that be above the heavens.
Let them praise the name of the Lord:
For he commanded, and they were created.
He hath also stablished them for ever and ever:
He hath made a decree which shall not pass.
Praise the Lord from the earth,
Ye dragons, and all deeps:
Fire, and hail; snow, and vapour;
Stormy wind fulfilling his word:
Mountains, and all hills;
Fruitful trees, and all cedars:
Beasts, and all cattle;
Creeping things, and flying fowl:
Kings of the earth, and all people;
Princes, and all judges of the earth:
Both young men, and maidens;
Old men, and children:
Let them praise the name of the Lord:
For his name alone is excellent;
His glory is above the earth and heaven.
He also exalteth the horn of his people,
The praise of all his saints;
Even of the children of Israel, a people near unto him.
Praise ye the Lord.

CL

Praise ye the Lord.
Praise God in his sanctuary:
Praise him in the firmament of his power.
Praise him for his mighty acts:
Praise him according to his excellent greatness.
Praise him with the sound of the trumpet:
Praise him with the psaltery and harp.
Praise him with the timbrel and dance:
Praise him with stringed instruments and organs.
Praise him upon the loud cymbals:
Praise him upon the high sounding cymbals.
Let every thing that hath breath praise the Lord.
Praise ye the Lord.

LOUIS UNTERMEYER, well-known poet, editor, short story writer and lecturer, has more than ninety volumes to his credit. His outstanding contributions to literature, especially in the field of poetry, have won him several honorary degrees and awards, including the Gold Medal of the Poetry Society of America. In 1961–1963, in recognition of his distinguished literary achievements, Mr. Untermeyer was appointed Consultant in Poetry to the Library of Congress.

The father of three sons, Mr. Untermeyer now lives with his wife in Newtown, Connecticut. When he is not engaged in literary activities, he indulges in his favorite pastimes which he lists as "puttering, planting, transplanting, playing the piano (sometimes) and continually playing with cats," of which there are six in the Untermeyer household.

JOAN BERG VICTOR, artist and book illustrator, is a graduate of H. Sophie Newcomb College and Yale University Graduate School of Art. A painter, draftsman, magazine illustrator, and designer, she has won many awards for her work. Mrs. Victor says that she loves the Psalms as pure poetry and has always wanted to illustrate them as she has done in this book, using only subjects from nature, celebrating the wonders of God's world. Her sensitive, delicate pencil drawings affirm the joyful tone of these beautiful poems. She and her husband and their son live in New York City.